PRAISE FOR
A NIGHT IN THE COUNTRY

Laura Newbern's *A Night in the Country* is at once direct and mysterious, a book of declarations and decrees subsumed in the language of the fable. These poems romp and turn and wander and wonder with no easy endings in sight, or as Newbern herself might say, "Life's a room: outside/it two great rivers meet in sunlight ... there is no help in them." These are exceptional poems, and a subtle song of heartbreak plays through every line.

—Jericho Brown

The poems in *A Night in the Country* contain poignant inquiries into the satisfactions that images provide, or fail to provide, in our mental and emotional lives. The poet imagines Renaissance painters at work; tries out various self-portraits with animals; resolves discrete images of daily life with an acknowledgement of the passionate distances and trade-offs involved in making art. She maintains a sort of visual staining in mind, so that the significance or resonance of a lyric moment must remain aesthetic, and not existential. In other words, the image houses the mixed feelings and unprovable intuitions that express the lyric impulse: "The mind goes back, the heart goes with it, the forest/whirls all around." Laura Newbern's poetry is the more remarkable because it makes these instances feel at once piercing and abidingly generous.

—Sandra Lim

There's a voice in this voice. You never want it to stop. But it's I who stopped, then quietly: *I love these poems.* Read this book. It will baffle. And get you through.

—Marianne Boruch

Published by Changes
www.changes.press

FIRST EDITION

Design by Studio Vance Wellenstein
Printing and binding by The John Roberts Company

Changes Paperback #003
ISBN 979-8-9889042-0-5
Library of Congress Control Number: 2023946165

A NIGHT IN THE COUNTRY
LAURA NEWBERN

FOREWORD BY
LOUISE GLÜCK

A CHANGES PAPERBACK

Changes

Also by Laura Newbern
Love and the Eye

FOREWORD

In the extraordinary opening poem of *A Night In The Country*, Laura Newbern imagines the painter Giovanni Bellini, or, more accurately, constructs a meditation around his obsessive renderings of the Madonna and Child. "Half his life," the poem says about the duration of the obsession. Over and over he paints these figures: context shifts, the emblems of holiness appear and vanish, until in the last canvas the figures are brought outside, into the world, where it appears that both painter and child realize the world this child is entering is not paradise but rather something more darkly ominous.

Bellini's restless returning to these figures is necessary because no single image can suffice, since any single image must exclude if it is to exist. The Madonna of the Meadow cannot also be the Madonna not of the Meadow. No one thing can be everything.

Poetry's impossible objectives—permanence, the dream of perfection—haunt these poems. Poems about art and the making of art recur, but in the main, *A Night in the Country* is rooted in a recognizable human reality, less rarefied than art but sharing with art a recognition of limitation. Dreamlike moments: a father writing to his daughters. A group of friends gathered in the woods for a memorial. Newbern treats limitation not as an occasion for rote mourning but as a subject for thought, a source of meaning. Despite their modest surfaces, these poems belong more to philosophy than to personal testament. Too oblique to be called intimate, they have intimacy's quietness and restraint, also its urgency. They read as someone thinking aloud, making careful adjustments and corrections in the interest of greater truth. Always Newbern favors the suggestive over the explicit, subtlety over bravura.

At a time when most are preoccupied with justice, with what can and must be changed, Laura Newbern writes about what does not change, writing not so much against current modes as apart from them. Small occasions, clear sentences. And underneath, measureless fathoms.

—Louise Glück

A Night
in the Country

Contents

I.

II.

for my parents, Barbara and David

the day at the window
the rain at the window
the night and the star at the window

—Robert Duncan, "The Fire, *Passages* 13"

I

Madonna of the Meadow

"Giovanni is very old and yet he is the best painter of all."

—Albrecht Dürer, 1506

The painter Bellini spent half his life
painting portraits of the Madonna.
Among other things.
In an early version she and the child
glow in a box of dark.
A little bit later, the painter admits
to clouds in the world, floating on either side
of the mother and child's world.
Later still, the Madonna lifts an apple with one hand
and cups the child in her lap with the other;
more importantly they are turned
to the right, just slightly, to where there is light
and, in the distance, a simple hill.
Until at last, in 1500, he brings the girl
and her burden outside, onto a field: bleak trees
on the left, a ragged chorus of clouds stealing
behind them, more hills, and a far
tower, looking like where they used to be.
He calls it a meadow, but there are hardly flowers,
and the clouds look like smoke belched
from the smokestacks—
but those are the trees. She wears

no halo. Holds the child there. Or rather
balances him, in her blue lap, where he seems
to sleep the sleep of an old man lost
at sea, and not in a meadow, not in a field at all.

The Walk

What if I dreamed of a plane that flew
onto a road, and traveled,
and landed itself at last
on the brown bank
of a river.

And if there were windows in back,
round and old-fashioned,
and I looking out, I
the lone passenger saw
the spindliest tree.

Hardly a tree
at all, in swamp winter—
more like a branching stick, like something
my grandfather on his long walk
might've brushed past, in his
waxed jacket—

There he is, on his long, lean walk
through life; there am I, my face
in the window, the window too thick
for sound, so I wave
my hand, in its
white glove …

And where did I read about planes
in dreams: you
are reaching your goals,
it said, or
you are dreaming of things
you cannot possibly do.

Self-Portrait with Water Rat

To make me, many people traveled a long way.
They traveled the Great River Road,
a wide and curving ribbon of sand
that runs alongside the deep and dividing river.

Hernando to Helena, Helena to
Marianna, Helena inland. Or out
to Napoleon, little river city filled with
gamblers and lawyers; city that drowned. They

were gamblers and lawyers, farmers and
owners of stores; men and women hauling themselves
out of the river and spreading,
like lights, into the fields.

There is no mirror here, in the lush land.
The wagon wheel rises in air.
And the water rat, in furs, on the bank, still there.
Holding its damp hand of cards.

Black Forest

Sometimes my mind goes back to certain things.
Like everyone's.
Like to the woman who asked me
What keeps you awake at night?
She wanted a writerly, magical answer.
A black forest, a shining maid walking through it.
The woman—she was a guest, a visiting artist.
I was a guest to her visitingness: polite guest
at an affable table.
My neck, I said, meaning pain
of the basest physical kind. Meaning also
sadness, and worry—
though I didn't say so.
I'd done enough, I'd said the neck thing
as if I were snapping a chicken for supper.
The woman smiled through it, a pro.
Oh, I'm sorry, she said, pushing the shining maid
into a closet and shutting the door in a hushed
and magical way.
I wanted to bind her with rope.
I wanted to watch her struggle, if just for a minute.
The mind goes back, the heart goes with it, the forest
whirls all around. Instead
I was kind to her husband, whose life
had had something to do with flight.

He was quiet, the husband. Like someone
whose part in the world was done.
He seemed to expect
no one.
He was the husband.
He was like light on the leaves of night.

Of the Mind

There were the days when Agatha Christie disappeared.
Even though she'd sent off a note, saying where she was.

There was her car, left at the lip of a pit, near a place
called the Silent Pool, which was said to be bottomless.

She was a suicide, said the papers. There was the car,
and the road, and the pit. There was even her dog—

brought to the scene, it stood there and whined.
And there were the men—so many—photographed

between trees, searching in groups, in their felts
and tweeds, in the silver gelatin trees, in the thin

woods. But it was not like Virginia Woolf; she was not
a body, prone in a river. She was upright, lodged

at one of the bigger, brighter spas in the country,
under her husband's lover's name. She was not

in the pit, not in the silent, bottomless pool.
And yet she was. Of course that was where she was.

Ashes

In the waiting room
I notice my doctor's a painter, his name scrawled
in the corner of a canvas depicting
two mountains, a country church, and a streaked sky.

And the painting is not on a wall
but on an easel thrust out like a hip
into the room, at hip level;

and on the TV overhead is a woman who wants to be
a millionaire, trying to decide
whether the Heaven Above Company is in the business
of placing a loved one's ashes inside a firework, or,
inside a stuffed animal.
C, or B. She cannot decide.

She cannot decide and the wait
is interminable; she wants it to be
B, stuffed animal; minutes and minutes go by
as she twists herself, in her striped shirt
and her denim jacket, into one answer and then
the other, smiling, grimacing, smiling again; she wants
that sweetness, maybe, even more than the money.

This is my country. My doctor
has painted the sky over his church a daring, devotional red
and I imagine my mother or maybe my beautiful red-headed sister
blazing across it: a starry final act.

And by then, at last, the woman contestant has it—reluctantly
C, she says, *final answer.* To which the host,
creating suspense, says, as slowly as possible, *You were all over the place,*
but you thought it through.
And you, my dear, yes. You came through.

Self-Portrait with Heron

Once, my mother tried to convince me
to have my portrait painted. Or to have *her*
have it—painted—: daughter of the house,

daughter on the wall, hanging daughter.
I might have worn a white dress, who knows.
I might have had my soul ensnared

in oils—if painters still do that—ensnare,
englobe … capture any small thing
(one feather, to please her—).

I might have worn a white dress, come out,
posed on the stairs of the house—
but I did not. I stood at the edge
of a small pond instead. A long time.

Cliffs and Hills

In the wax museum, John Brown lies in a bed.
Wax Brown, real bed; but the bed
a low prison-cot, Brown being still
too wounded to rise and walk.

Nor is there any glass between you
and him and the soldiers guarding him
in their dark cloaks, in their moth wool;
their faces a sallow yellow, their wax
expressions grim atop their stiffly
arranged bodies; one looks down, another twists
slightly away. Only Brown, a shine on his face
from a light somewhere in the ceiling,
looks straight up at heaven. Or heaven
looks down, through a hole, on him.

Next scene: Brown leans
against the gallows-ladder and the room
is blue as night. And Brown looks hale,
upright; and once again a light
brightens all that's him: long beard,
face on fire—when you arrived
you saw it burning in a window ...

And those soldiers' poses—who
would take such a dying man, thin
as a strap, a man aglow, to the dread
gallows? Oh, not they. Their shoulders,
pressed as bentwood chairs and
hunkered so—
their shoulders know.

Life's a room: outside it
two great rivers meet in sunlight;
cliffs rise up and turn to hills that roll away
like greenish waves; there is no help
in them. There's only endless
blue-brown river.
Bristling day.

Asylum Pastoral, or, Happiness

Here, across the big lawn, and over the dome, the gray in the sky
is expanding, gently and slowly outward, and all over Georgia today
it is going to rain.

And in the story last night
which I read to you in the tenderest voice I could muster

the peasants stood by a pond, with the filthy ducks and the slick lilies,
and rain, rain
was coming. The men in the story were bathing: two in the bathhouse,
one in the terrible pond; the one who would not tolerate
silence, complacency,
     took to the pond and the oncoming rain. And when I asked you

"was it too grim,"
I meant to be funny; I meant you are dear
to me. And here, where so many suffered, and suffered alone, here
     to my left
are a greenish awning, great corroding columns, two doves
diving in ivy, and spots of brass in the sky—dull drums
of brightness, promising
something. Health, love …

     unbridled silence and stillness. One cannot hear
the past, or manage the future,

but sitting, back to a tree, watching the slight light shift on a
bronzed cupola, feel

one moment's happiness—*last night I read*
to you—and in the turning breeze
the rain that is coming; the cool of the pond as it must have felt
to the man, Iván, who in his restlessness
and in his delaying the girl who would bring him kindness, and sleep,
reminds me of you.

Like a candle, like happiness:
        so she moves through the pages.

Email From My Father

"Daughters," my father writes,
and at a stroke
I am the spaniel
curled on a shawl,
by a low fire if you didn't
notice, before—
possibly hard to see
in the andiron glow,
in the lush soot
there was more of—

"Daughters," my father
writes, to myself
and my sister, as if
he were a preacher
in a long frock, under a bough
laden with apples; so
my father tends to begin:
"Daughters,"—

And there is conjured
a plain chair, in a warmed
room; there are a chair
and a wall and a bowl,
and a window through which

you can muster the sea—
a flash, a glimpse—
through the black trees.

Then, there, I circle myself and
sink to the word, silky of ear and
true, to the bone.

And my sister—younger, red-headed, white-capped—
out sailing,
into the future.

Summer Afternoon

Those are the words of the writer, the one who deemed them
the two most beautiful words in the English
language—*summer* and *afternoon*. But who of course
loved not the words, but what they conjured.
For him, maybe, it was his man, with a tray, descending
a slope of lawn in a black suit; and he himself
in a simple chair, in the shade; but an upholstered
chair, an inside chair brought out, and the shade
the shade of a great sleeping tree. I read a novel
in which a man who had done something terrible stole
away, in a boat no one had noticed, having descended
a cliff, away from a great house and all the way down
to a river, all the way down to an also unnoticed dock
where the boat floated, in wait. And dark clouds
raced down the river—not the word *dark*, nor
the word *clouds*, but the fact of the secret boat now
in the open; the man crouched inside it, escaping; the current
ample, the ancient trees on either bank forming
a hallway of sunset, laced with smoke: dark clouds, dark clouds.

Night Road

"Tristan," she said, when I asked her
the name of the cat she'd been
talking about, the one
who was so needy, who needed
always to be in her lap,
who would wail like a child
when he was not. We were driving—
sometimes there is nothing to do
but drive—we were speeding along
on the road by the water,
the silent water, which, at night,
is invisible. Almost invisible—
calm, glassy, a slice of moon
flashing it for us here and there,
letting us know where we were,
though we knew well
the body of water and even better
the strip of land running beside it—
sparse houses, single stars,
the dark board of the straight road
and the white clapboard church that
heaves itself, up
out of the ground—"Tragic,"
I said, which came out a bit
as funny, but real, but meant.

By day that body of water is
deeply blue; by night it is black,
as a charm. By day King Mark
in his paper crown stood on the
shore and wondered who
had taken his love ... by night, he knew.

A Night in the Country

Last night—mild, September—
my friend of twenty years strung lights
in a forest of cedars.
Not quite a forest—a gathering of trees
close to the road, behind a historic cabin
and only a stone's throw from his
mother's house—his mother who died
one year ago; thus the lights, neighbors,
family, friends, and even a two-man band
under the trees.

Prayer, then food: the oldest among us
sat themselves down at the tables when they were told.
And the rest of us, younger but not so young
anymore, stood in the shadows, drinking
and talking; drinking from wineglasses there
in the mild wood, feeling
for the first time the weight
of the dark, the way night
weighs and falls. It is nice

to have glasses and silver and china plates
in the open, the middle of nowhere, that far out
in the country. Silvery moths
the size of hands landed upon us.

True dark and the band struck up, and one of the oldest men
jumped up and danced a jig and just before doing it screamed
I can dance! And my friend's partner of ten years
or so (I hadn't seen them since the funeral) said
Sometimes out here, I'm afraid ... Think, he said,
of the Quakers who settled this place
(a church and the cabin are all that remain);
their cattle, he said, *their cattle were*
their lives, and they had no lights ... This
under the strung lights, toward the end of the night,
the old men and the relatives having by then
shuffled off to their cars and
home, to bed. *Scary,* he said, lifting his
graying head to the so many moons
on their invisible strings.
The two-man band had gone, too; it seems to me now
that they bowed their heads as they walked away.

And I did, I thought of the Quakers, there
in their gray frocks, walking the worn paths
still to be seen under the cedars; navigating
the monstrous dark, trunk by trunk.
Oh they had lanterns, and candles—

but still. And now my friend, still bereaved,
stumbling, exhausted, tipping to sleep and gone

white in the face—
he looks like his mother, who lived
out in that country alone. Who kept goats
in a low pen, close to the house. They must have sometimes
cried in the night; she must have risen,
turned on the light, remembering where
the telephone was, a hand
on the wall ... Those lights—

they seemed to grow brighter, tree to tree.
And the later, the darker it got, the more there were Quakers,
gray girls and boys and mothers and fathers, moving.
All they wanted was family, peace.
And from that, from that place, they were driven away.

Christmas

A man gives a woman a book
of full-color photographs
of the Delta.
It's big and it's square;
it shines on the table, under a lamp.
She looks at it when the man
is not looking: cotton fields yawning
into a watery sun, sunflowers turning
their gawky tattered heads to a pale horizon.
Small planes at the edges of fields.

She hates it—the book—it's a
rip-off, a heavy, touristy thing, an advertisement
for light—but quietly loves
the photos, the thorned trunks
of the cypress-dwarves, the green
of their homely ponds; the silvery lift
of a thousand silver birds, caught—

When he is not looking, not home,
she stares at a close-up
of a cotton boll.
It was left behind in a field.
And it looks
like a walnut, giving birth to a cloud.

II

Dürer's Self-Portrait

In the woods,
the young hare
and the squirrel
tend to the low
flora, while
he sits for himself
in Italian party clothes
in a tower.
Hair streaming down,
twin rivers.
And in the tower window
are painted fields,
neat, Provençal,
and green hills,
and the one cloud
casting about
for a direction.
The hare and the squirrel
meanwhile—
meanwhile the pooling eyes
of the little owl—
everything says
Albrecht, one day
you too will head for the woods.

Country Night

My mother's father was hard on my mother's mother.
I know this, but knowing means nearly nothing; the man,
seen by me, was a tall man, wearing a hat
in the old way, standing beside the open
door of a car, on a dust road.
Like a sentence, the poem is half
in sunlight, half in shadow; sometimes cloaked
in a dark night: my grandfather driving,
Nat King Cole on the radio and
my grandmother humming along.
I'm in the back, little, and so in love
with him, and with her, and with the pines
rising up and away on either side,
and how he would say as we rode through the dark
a wolf is going to come out of those trees and eat you. I know
that is a story for children; I know
my grandmother hummed like a warbler, yellow glow
in the deep wood, for most of her life.
Her throat brimming with sunlight.

Frankenstein at the Table

1.

This morning my rooms, my street
were quiet as always
except for the voices of women
out walking, one
saying *I'm proud of you* to the other and
somewhere in the offing
a screaming child.

2.

At the table, in the old film, it's all
so nice, for a time—
the old man doesn't mind
Frankenstein's growling; they sit
in that rich black-and-white light
together, a minute.
It's 1935. And then
it all goes to hell.

3.

Outside
it is a Saturday still
beginning; dead-end of summer, no cars

moving. I can hear
everything—leaves, and the lack
of birds. And the sunlight
scissoring now; that sharp
casting of shadows, already starting—

4.

Is it a girl at the river,
holding a gray daisy,
a flower for chains,
out and over the water?

5.

In the book,
the old man has a family,
a daughter and son
who dote on him.
They work an old farm.
They are poor
but their world is silver;
evening comes
and they read to each other.

6.

No music, quiet
yellow and white morning ...
The river is blocks away but someone
is already there filming
the stones in their gray hoods

And Frankenstein sits at the table, his soup
before him. His weighted shoes
on the floor.

7.

Think of it: how much the animal,
bored in its stall, gathers in
of your comings and goings;
how you might shoulder a thing on your back
and leave, into the field of summer,
or into the cave of winter,
and how you return, heard,
then seen, through a hole
in the wood ...

8.

And before there was ever a table,
Frankenstein stood
outside the hovel, ear to the door; leaning
a little bit forward, a little bit
back—

9.

Here there's a river
but this is no country
of ice or crag; the distances
flat; the sun in the morning
gauzy as movie gold.

I looked for a friend;
this is what I wrote.

Novella

On the last day of summer
    there was a man by the river.

We were the women, gathered
    for wine on the rocks: there were three

or four of us, eyes on each other and
    on the river. Sunlight

dazzled the water, small knives
    making their final cuts

on the rush and void. We talked,
    we made noise; we had things to say—

And then he was there, the man
    by the river, crouched

on the slaty shelf at our backs,
    drunk, we could tell, but not frightening;

drunk in the way of the true drunk,
    sullen and still, and silent,

until he said, quite loud,
      he had a *girl*, who was *lonely*,

back at the motel, so could she maybe
      join you ladies. All of us

looked in the same direction, then.
      We whispered, without saying words.

We all looked across, to the river's
      bar: small, sandy, bedraggled island,

uninhabited, ashen—seeing
      a gray two-lane, a sign, a stand

of leaning pines; maybe a hand,
      parting the curtains—

There was a man, we said of it later,
      in our bright kitchens filled with

glass, *down by the river*; nobody said
      that there was a girl or even

fully imagined her—did we?
    —Not until later, the river already

winter-dull and the maples
    practically bare, gone deep into fall.

The Burning West

Every fire has a name.
Today, the Detwiler fire, which sounds
like someone tentative but intent, someone
at the door. Hello?
It's the Detwiler fire.

Herr Detweiler—that was the name
of the Von Trapps' eager promoter
in *The Sound of Music.* In which
the baroness used to be bad—I mean, I used to think
she was awful; now I understand
and even admire her veils, her perfected hair.
She wanted a husband, a beautiful home;
she wanted those urns on either side
of the view of the river,
the handsome captain standing there with her.

But no one's so safe. Out west
the mountains are veiled in smoke, the cool
mountains, the swirling Pacific and all its mists
too far away. Not near enough.
Von Schraeder—

so was the baroness named: Elsa von Schraeder.
Maria, you might remember, had no name

besides Maria; a simple name, and a simple blue dress
like a small, wayward flame—

You could see it through all the trees.

Myth

Somebody asked me, straightforwardly, *What*
is your mythology?
What? I said, meaning, what do you mean—I didn't understand
the question. Though I remember I thought I should. Understand.

It was a man who asked me, someone
I didn't know well, but knew to respect—
a teacher, and old. He had a fluff of white hair
and he leaned way back in his chair.

We sat at a table for two. I thought of trees—
the oaks and big elms that shaded the street
I grew up on. Then—I had a glass of red wine
in my hand—I thought of my grandfather, whose name

was Charles, and how, after his stroke, the priest
brought the goblet to him and knelt with him
on the living room floor; they did the whole service
over the coffee table, which, likely, was soothing.

And it may be that I thought of my other grandfather,
John, John Allen, who kept his bird-hunting dogs
in a cage of silvery wire, at the back of the back yard;
all the way back, where I was afraid

to go, for all the slathering tongues, and noses pressing
on air—*what next, what next.* The man, the teacher,
was pleased with his question, I could tell; it had a
mission. I summoned an answer, polite. I followed my grandfather
      out to the silver-and-wire edge

of all that was real, while my grandmother, cautious woman,
counted the redbirds alighting right there in her window.

Fables and Seas

Once, my father sent me a wondrous letter.
About a night when my parents were truly
young; when he and my mother, traveling together

in Europe, drove into Luxembourg and knew
they needed, without reservations, a place
to stop for the night. We had you

with us, he wrote, and at the late
hour, at the inn with its last
room, the owners worried over the baby—

baby crying all night, in the blue bath-
light of Luxembourg, your parents
young as they were. So we wrapped

you up, tight, my father wrote, bent
over whatever crib was provided, over
the glass globe now in a letter

composed, and sent: the little red car
parked outside ...
You did not make a sound, he wrote, from a far

place, but close, and clear as ice. All night
it snowed. Like a bright ghost in the gorges.

Iliad

Hector dies.
You are eleven or twelve and proud
to know his name, to be able to name
Hector, and others, in front of your beautiful teacher.
Maybe that's why
it was so good, then; you remember
loving the long lists and hearing the verse
with pleasure—whatever, when one is twelve,
or eleven, pleasure is; you could name
all the gods and goddesses, all the weeping
mothers and fathers, all
who wept, clutching their chests, for Hector, dead.

Her name—teacher, goddess, was Mrs. Givan, and what
she must have given to row upon row of girls
over the years you can begin, now,
to imagine. And never mind the girl
in the front who with a yellow pencil steadily dug
and tasted the wax from her ear; you
with your studious face could stay, all afternoon,
in the dust of Hector's terrible dragging,
filled with admiring.

What was weeping, anyway, then?
A gesture, an illustration, something locked

behind the black double doors of the house you
came striding out of, mornings, wearing your uniform
of blazer and high socks, and the pressed
skirt ...

You could not see it, not quite,
in the woman standing
in warm classroom light.
Soft brown hair.
Standing there, reading to children.

Starry Night

My great-grandfather was an astronomer.
I never saw him.
These winter nights, I do not know
what is out there.
I know that the bare trees in front of the house
soar into space, and that in space
it is dark, and cold.
I like to think
he drove a black car that purred
when he nosed it around the corner,
approaching his home,
and that he drove slowly, like a cortege.
Those trees I mentioned are thin
and Orion rises behind them and stays
a long time. The black car
slides down the block, and everyone knows
who it is: he wrote a book and called it
Astronomy, and for his portrait
wore a gray suit and posed like a banker.
When I'd pass by it the oils would flare
and the eyes would go white
and, for a moment, he would look blind.
It was a heavy book, *Astronomy*, bound
in the way of old books.
The pages shone.
The cover was navy blue.

Self-Portrait with Wolf

When I was a child I believed in everything.
I believed that you
were the sound of a horn ... yellowed, magisterial
air that could move the leaves
at the edge of the pond.

And that what you ate
could sing inside you.

And more—that the song, sad, head-hung,
coming from some lightless place,
could be heard by others.
But mostly, principally, by me.

This is the way, as I stand in the field,
facing the wall-edge of the woods,
I listen for you.
First for the gleaming note.
Then for a voice.

In every story
somebody shoots you—a long gun, the woods
in winter, whitened field, spot of blood, the trailing off, then,
of the sun—

and then that story becomes my life.

If I could just draw what I am, what we are,
instead of saying it—

edge-grass of the field, russet; the trees
smudging up into tree line, like crowns of smoke—

I love you; I love also what dies
in you, whatever
small, swallowed creature. That is why
everything's still; why
I stand alone in the picture.

No hunter walking out of the woods, carrying you
over his shoulder.
Only the light's low brass.

Ghazal

(*The Ecstasy of St. Francis*)

In Bellini's sweet painting, St. Francis looks out on the country.
Shoes off, open-mouthed, he's lost to the light of the country.

Landscape, desert—everything glows; everything
turns to a rose, in the heart of the country.

What burning bush wouldn't burn, in so much placidity?
A far tower, some sheep—what you find in that part of the country.

God's still alive, say the animals; look
to our double lanterns, our eyes, in the night, in the country.

St. Francis leans back, as on an invisible bluff of air: breath
of the moon and the sun. And to his right there's a donkey.

The painting wound up in New York, in the velvety living room of an
     old man.
Fifth Avenue, carriages, snow and sleet ... pink fire in a firelit country.

I pray to St. Francis, when I have to pray, because he seems
kind and astonished and stricken by everything: true saint of the country.

Even the laurel tree, tasseled with dawn, leans into the frame.
It leans to the man in the country. The art, the humility.

Self-Portrait with Dog

In the grocery store
by the soup
I burst into tears
and for no reason
other than you,
so large and so brown
and in your burgundy service vest
right by your person,
who was not blind
but was slow-moving.

Soup is good
on a day like this
when in late afternoon
it is dark already;
one comes to depend
on things like a stove
or a lamp,
or a round rug,
or a dog.

And what a mess we've made
of the world.

Do not look up at me;
I cannot fix it,

nor can you lead me out of it—
not your job.

You must go home.
I, too, must go home.

Sycamore

They say when you die
your mother comes to get you. I write "They say"
and a bevy of women, ancient, diminutive,
dressed in black capes and caps, gather—
not in a room but outdoors, maybe
on the *campagna* of Rome, before there was Rome.
They say, they say, they say.

When my own mother said it to me
in a voice that was skeptical, but clear;
low and foreboding, but with a strip of hope,
we were walking around on the farm
and we'd come to the place where a sycamore
lords it over the creek; grows straight out of a hill
and leans over water and rocks. You can tell
a sycamore tree by its white trunk—
in a winter landscape, it is the ghost.
My mother, always a little ahead of me.

And in the fields of Rome ...

Birds, I imagine. Circling,
seeking the tree that has bared itself.
And the one bird who decides to find it.

The Veil

It is said, now, that the last painting Van Gogh undertook
wasn't the crows in the field
but was a painting of roots of trees
growing out of the side of a hill, on a curve
leading into Auvers-sur-Oise, or out of it, and
just meters from where he was staying, from the small room
with its chair, the room in which he would die.

And there was an unveiling, of the spot, of the roots
still alive in the side of the hill, as they were, still there—
(where would they go?). The director
of the museum attended; she came from Amsterdam and
stood, in a skirt, good shoes, right there in the road.
Hands clasped, I suppose.

Did someone cover the roots, the trees, the whole side of the hill
with a white veil and then
expose them? How do you unveil
what has been there a hundred years,
and thirty more after that—roots and
earth the painter rendered in greens and blues.

Here's an old photo, of the auberge Van Gogh
went home to, every evening, in the last months—
the owners posed outside, good proprietors,

leaning away in their aprons. One stick-table; two stick-chairs ...
and, at center, in the dark doorway, one young woman,
likely the daughter, broom in hand,
staring into forever. Oh stock-still. Straight ahead.

NOTES

"Madonna of the Meadow" owes a debt to John Berger's essay on Giovanni Bellini in his book *Portraits*.

"Summer Afternoon" references E. L. Doctorow's novel *The Waterworks*. Henry James is the writer who loved the words "summer" and "afternoon."

"Asylum Pastoral, or, Happiness" references Anton Chekhov's story "Gooseberries."

"A Night in the Country" is for John McBrayer and Rich Howe.

"Novella" is for Sue Hennessy, Dorothy Pilloni, and Zita Leonard.

ACKNOWLEDGMENTS

Thanks are due to the editors of the following publications, in which some of these poems first appeared, some in different versions:

Barrow Street ("Madonna of the Meadow," "The Burning West"), *The Massachusetts Review* ("Of the Mind"), *New England Review* ("Ashes," "Fables and Seas," "Summer Afternoon"), *Plume* ("Black Forest," "Country Night"), and *The Southern Review* ("Iliad"). "Novella" originally appeared in the anthology *Why I Wrote This Poem*, edited by William Walsh.

Thanks also to Bennet Bergman for his vision, and to everyone at Changes for their faith in this book; to Jonathan Blunk for his kind encouragement and sharp eye; and to those who provided the gift of space or time, especially the Rona Jaffe Foundation, Pam Kukla and Tom O'Hearn, Parkman Howe and Melinda Lindquist, and Doug Oetter of Upland Meadows.

And to Louise Glück, whose keen attention to these poems I have learned from, and will continue to learn from, my unending gratitude.

ABOUT THE AUTHOR

Laura Newbern comes from two long lines of Arkansans, was born in Germany, and grew up in Washington, D.C. Her first book, *Love and the Eye*, was selected by Claudia Rankine for the Kore Press First Book Award, and she's the recipient of a Writer's Award from the Rona Jaffe Foundation.

She lives in Georgia and teaches at Georgia College and at Reinhardt University.